A Touch of Rose Madder

A Play

Jim O'Connor

A SAMUEL FRENCH ACTING EDITION

SAMUEL FRENCH

FOUNDED 1830

SAMUELFRENCH-LONDON.CO.UK
SAMUELFRENCH.COM

FOR AMATEUR PRODUCTION ENQUIRIES

UNITED KINGDOM AND WORLD
EXCLUDING NORTH AMERICA
plays@SamuelFrench-London.co.uk
020 7255 4302/01

Each title is subject to availability from Samuel French,

depending upon country of performance.

CHARACTERS

Rose Carlyle, a widow, early 70s
Danny Carlyle, Rose's son, 40s
Leslie Wilkinson, Rose's Home Help, late 20's/30's

The action of the play takes place in Rose's bedroom-cum-sitting room

Time — the present

NOTE

At the author's express request, *A Touch of Rose Madder* does not conform to French's house style for Acting Editions.

A TOUCH OF ROSE MADDER

SCENE 1

Rose's room

It is a modestly but comfortably furnished room with a door leading from it to a hallway and kitchen. One of the walls has a fireplace in it; the mantelpiece has an old carriage clock (now stopped) a flute and family photos on it. US are a single made-up bed, a clothes rail and a bedside cabinet with a light on it. Elsewhere there is a TV set with a chair pulled up close to it; the telephone is nearby, within reach

The play begins in darkness. We hear a plaintive air on a flute. The Lights come up in the room. The music fades

Danny Carlyle is hanging a framed watercolour beach scene above the bed. He stands back to check the position, arranges the pillow on the bed, tests the bedside light, then lifts the phone and dials

Danny (*into the phone*) B6 please. ... Hallo, it's Mr Carlyle. Could you tell my mother I'll be there in an hour. ... How is she today? ... Excited. ... And a few tears. Well, it's been a long time for her hasn't it? ... Yes I'll be here for a few days to settle her in ... OK then, I'll see you shortly. Thanks. (*He replaces the phone. He moves to the clock, adjusts its hands and tilts it but it remains stopped*)

Danny exits, his tasks completed

The Lights fade

SCENE 2

Two weeks later. Saturday, 10 a.m.

The bed is now unmade. Some pills are scattered on the floor and Rose's dressing-gown is across the end of her bed

The Lights come up. The sound of a radio comes from the kitchen. It stops

Seconds later Rose Carlyle enters. She is wearing a bright tracksuit and carpet slippers and pushing a trolley on which are a slice of buttered toast, a mug of tea, a long-arm gripper rod, a reading glass, a box of tissues and some pills; a lower shelf has a jumble of objects including an envelope on it. Rose's progress towards her chair is slow as she has obvious limited mobility. Halfway across the room the trolley jars, causing the toast to fall onto the carpet

Rose (*surveying the carpet*) Bugger it! Now where did that go! (*She bends slightly, thinks better of it and instead takes the gripper rod from the trolley. She peers at the floor, locates the toast and, smiling, raises it a few feet from the floor*)

The doorbell rings

Rose drops the toast

There is a second ring on the doorbell

Rose gives up and, ignoring the second ring on the doorbell, completes the journey to her chair, clearly frustrated

Leslie (*off*) Hallo. … Hallo. … Mrs Carlyle.
Rose In here.
Leslie (*off*) Hallo.
Rose For God's sake. (*Louder*) Come in then!

Leslie appears carrying a bottle of milk, a loaf of bread and his personal bag

Leslie Are you all right, everything OK?
Rose I could do with a megaphone.
Leslie Sorry … I didn't want to walk straight in.
Rose (*noting the milk and loaf*) Is Albert off today?
Leslie Albert? I think he's been and gone. These were inside the door.
Rose I wanted to catch him. I hope that's not thin sliced again.
Leslie Did you know your door was open?
Rose He usually gives me a shout.
Leslie And you're all right?
Rose Yes, still above ground. Who are you then?
Leslie I'm Leslie, Mrs Carlyle.

No reaction

Leslie Wilkinson.

Still no reaction

Rose Should that ring a bell with me?
Leslie I was hoping it would. I'm from the Social Services. Sorry I'm a bit late.
Rose Late for what?
Leslie Didn't they get in touch with you, phone, tell you I was coming?
Rose I can't always get to the phone. You're from the Social Services?
Leslie That's right.
Rose Have you come to finish my grip?
Leslie Grip?
Rose My hand grip. Someone came last week, put two up in the kitchen, drilled the holes for one in my toilet and I haven't seen him since. That's the one I need. I'm all right going down, coming up's the trouble.

Leslie I'm afraid they didn't tell me anything about that.

Rose Oh I know, I rang about Brenda.

Leslie Brenda? Ah, she has you during the week doesn't she?

Rose No, she doesn't.

Leslie No?

Rose No, I have her. Not that it was my idea.

Leslie But she is your Home Help.

Rose Help! She spends most of her time doing keep fit with my vacuum cleaner. It's her that needs help. I can tell you a lot about Brenda, and her husband, and her boyfriend. You seem to employ anybody these days.

Leslie I wouldn't say that.

Rose Her time-keeping could improve for a start. Late in and early out, that's your Brenda. I've told her any more monkey business and she can go climb a tree.

Leslie I've not come to check on Brenda Mrs Carlyle.

Rose You haven't?

Leslie No. But I understand she won't be coming any more.

Rose Been sacked has she or turned it in?

Leslie I just know you won't be seeing her again. And as far as I can gather neither will her husband.

Rose I wonder if he's as pleased as I am.

Leslie So the office didn't tell you about her replacement?

Rose Replacement! Oh no, no thanks, not any more, I've had quite enough, thank you. I told my son I didn't want strange women coming into my house in the first place. No you tell 'em, I can manage on my own; I won't be needing anyone else.

Leslie I'm afraid it's a little late for that.

Rose If they're sending one she'll do an about-turn on the step.

Leslie I can guarantee you definitely won't be having another Brenda — at least over the weekend.

Rose They're not sending anybody then?

Leslie Yes … They've — already sent someone.

There is a pause as this slowly sinks in

Rose Already sent …

Leslie Do you think this milk ought to go in the fridge?
Rose Now just a minute sonny, you hold it right there. Are you telling me you're my Home Help?
Leslie No-one else seemed to be available over the weekend.
Rose Got a reputation, have I?
Leslie Perhaps you ought to telephone the office but I promise you it's all above board.
Rose Who says? Nobody asked me. What do they think I am?
Leslie (*placing the bread and milk on the trolley*) According to your assessment, an elderly person who since returning from hospital requires some domestic assistance.
Rose But I've told them, all of them, I don't need their assistance. This is all down to Danny isn't it? He did this.
Leslie Who's Danny?
Rose My son. It's bad enough having "Meals On Wheels". I've told him a dozen times I don't want that van outside my house.
Leslie It sounds as if he's looking after your interests.
Rose I'd like to decide what I eat and when. The neighbours can find something else to gossip about. God knows what they'd think of you.
Leslie I could be your doctor.
Rose You came by car did you?
Leslie No, I — cycled here.
Rose Cycled! Like all doctors do these days.
Leslie Do you see much of your neighbours Mrs Carlyle?
Rose Not if I can help it.
Leslie Well then, what does it matter what they think. Let their imaginations run riot. Have some fun at their expense.
Rose (*brightly*) I suppose you could be my lodger.
Leslie If you like …
Rose Or maybe a relative ——
Leslie Why not …
Rose — visiting for a while ——
Leslie Could be …
Rose — or even my toy-boy coming and going …
Leslie Now you're talking …
Rose Don't be so bloody daft! On yer bike.

Leslie You don't want me to stay then?
Rose Would you like two words of advice!
Leslie OK, fair enough. (*He produces his cycle clips from his bag and puts them on*)

There is the sound of distant thunder

No point in flogging a dead horse.
Rose Dead horse! You cheeky bugger! If I had the strength I'd march you to the door myself.
Leslie I didn't mean … What I meant was you're obviously a — woman who knows her own mind, that's all.
Rose And you tell 'em. I'm not doolally yet.
Leslie I can see that. I suppose I'd feel the same in your situation.
Rose What do you know about my situation.
Leslie Look, I'm sorry if I ——

The thunder sounds again, closer now

— said anything to … (*He takes a cap from his bag and puts it on*) Before I leave though could I ask you to sign my sheet, just to verify that I've been here? If you like you can add a note to say you don't want any more calls. They'll have it in black and white then won't they?
Rose Not from me they won't.
Leslie I can drop it in today.
Rose I don't write any more. Didn't they tell you anything about me?
Leslie A little.
Rose What do they know.

There is the sound of heavy rain; this continues throughout the scene

Haven't you got a cape?
Leslie I didn't think I'd need one.
Rose Sit down a minute, I can't send you out in that can I.

Leslie It's probably only a shower. (*He sits*)
Rose When I was young I won prizes for handwriting, for style and presentation. Now I can barely recognise my own signature.
Leslie Some would say that's a sign of intelligence.
Rose Not those who've had a stroke. (*She drinks her tea, which has obviously gone cold*)
Leslie Why don't I put the kettle on for you, make you a fresh pot?
Rose I suppose you could drink one could you?
Leslie I think I could. I take it you've had some breakfast?
Rose My breakfast? Oh yes, I've had that.
Leslie What was it, something nice?
Rose Well, first thing I usually put a teabag in a mug and ——
Leslie You're like me then, you need your tea to get going, eh? What else?
Rose What else? Oh cereal, then some toast, and I put an egg on with a couple of rashers ——
Leslie Mmmm that's nice …
Rose — a tin of beans, a fried tomato and a handful of mushrooms with a few potatoes and fried bread and ——
Leslie You do all that!
Rose Trouble is … The trouble is …
Leslie What Mrs Carlyle?
Rose I never know what to have for the main course.
Leslie I didn't think you did all that.
Rose No, not now. I did though for years, three times over. They didn't go outside the door without a good breakfast inside them.
Leslie As long as you've had something. Let me clear these for you. (*He picks up the piece of toast from the floor*) Did you have some toast?
Rose I dropped that while I was juggling. There's a few of my pills down there as well.

Leslie, on the floor, searches round and finds a few pills

Leslie I'd better get to know your kitchen.
Rose You're only making tea, it's all on the table.

Leslie makes to move off into the kitchen with the trolley

Leave that, I need that.

Leslie gathers up the breakfast items, the bread and milk and heads for the kitchen

Would you see if the postman's been. And the paperboy.
Leslie Right. Back in a second.

Leslie exits

Rose searches through the odd items on the trolley's lower shelf and finds the envelope. She peers closely at it. She looks again at the lower shelf

Leslie returns from the hallway with the mail and a newspaper

Leslie Kettle's on and there's your post and paper.

Leslie hands the envelopes and newspaper to Rose

Rose You found everything.
Leslie Yes, no problem. There's nothing lacking in your kitchen, is there. I like your stove, very modern.
Rose Danny put that in while I was away. If I'd known I'd have told him to save the money, I was happy with gas.
Leslie Electric is safer.
Rose You know that do you.
Leslie I know you don't have to light it.
Rose We had electric in the hospital, I couldn't get on with it there. I like a flame I can see.
Leslie They got you cooking did they?
Rose Boiling a kettle, beans on toast. Hardly cooking is it?
Leslie I'll fetch the tea.
Rose Can you see my reading glass?
Leslie (*finding the reading glass on top of the trolley*) Here it is.

Rose The time I spend searching for things that are right in front of me ...

Leslie exits

There's some biscuits in the tin.

The phone rings. Rose answers it

(*Into the phone*) Hallo. ... I've been waiting for you to ring. ... No, I was tossing and turning. It's not the same sleeping down here. ... No she's not coming any more. ... Oh yes they sent somebody else all right and this one's nothing like Brenda. ... It doesn't matter Danny, it's the last visit, I'm not having any more. ... Where are you now then? ... Well you'd better get a move on, they only do an hour. ... Yes, I've had my pills. (*She hangs up the phone, searches the trolley top, finds a pill and pops it into her mouth*)

Leslie returns with a tray of tea items and biscuits. He places the tray on the trolley and pours tea for both of them

Rose That's my Danny; says he'd like to have a word with you.
Leslie He's on his way, is he?
Rose He's in traffic, not far.
Leslie I've poured the tea. Sugar's there.
Rose What did you say your name was?
Leslie Leslie.
Rose You've got a few of us on your list have you, sweet old ladies like me?
Leslie Just you for the weekend.
Rose I suppose some need you more than most. I don't, I've got a full fridge and freezer. Danny sees to that.
Leslie He looks after you, doesn't he?
Rose He thinks so. (*She takes a biscuit*) These are nice. Go on have one.
Leslie Thanks.

Rose The morning trolley came round at ten-thirty, always ten-thirty. I was ready for it I can tell you, especially after the physio had finished with me. It was good food in there, lots of variety, and hot. Once I got my appetite back I always finished my plate. Not like Elsie next to me, she hardly touched a thing poor soul. Her husband always polished off her meals. He used to sit there ticking the menu for the next day, I never once heard him asking Elsie what she wanted. (*She drains her mug*) Well now, I enjoyed that.

Leslie There's more tea in the pot if you'd like one.

Rose No, it'll only have me running outside.

Leslie I can help if you need me.

Rose You! That'll be the day.

Leslie I've done it before.

Rose Where?

Leslie In the hospital where I was a nurse.

Rose You're a nurse!

Leslie I've seen it all Mrs Carlyle, men's wards, women's, geriatrics, you name it.

Rose What are you doing here then?

Leslie They closed it, merged it with another twenty miles away.

Rose Cut it you mean.

Leslie They called it "rationalizing the service".

Rose Call it what you like, another hospital that was there isn't now.

Leslie I could have gone to the new one but I needed a change so I came down to London and signed on with the agency.

Rose And was Brenda from your agency?

Leslie No. They tend to call on us more at weekends, to cover emergencies.

Rose I am not an emergency! How many times … I know it's not your fault, but — I was so looking forward to coming back to my own house and getting into the old routines.

Leslie It's early days yet. You can't expect to do things too soon.

Rose Run before I can walk. I suppose so. I took a few months before I could even do that. I honestly thought I'd make it upstairs, I could hardly get up the front step.

Leslie You'll get there in time.

Rose They don't think so.

Leslie Who?
Rose The hospital told Danny I'd never come back.
Leslie You can't live with him?
Rose What in Birmingham! Bugger Birmingham! I wouldn't if he had room. This is my home.
Leslie You must of been here a few years.
Rose Since it was built, nineteen-thirties. Fifteen hundred pounds then. Makes you think doesn't it?
Leslie You're sure you don't want more tea?
Rose No, you can clear this lot. Just leave it in the kitchen.
Leslie I'll wash it up, no trouble.
Rose Leave it. The exercise is good for me.

Leslie exits to the kitchen with the tray

Rose looks at the mail

Leslie returns without the tray

Rose Is it still raining?
Leslie No, it seems to have cleared up.
Rose (*indicating the mail*) You can help me with these before you go.

Leslie sits near Rose and takes the mail from her

What have I got there then?
Leslie It's an interesting selection. (*He opens an envelope*)
Rose Like what?
Leslie Well now Mrs Carlyle, do you want to (*he reads*) "Shape up, Slim down and Transform your body with the Betty Conlon Diet and Fitness Club"?
Rose In the bin. What else?
Leslie (*reading another letter*) "Thinking of buying your first home? Because the Nationwide Building Society are offering you, as a first time buyer, a free step by step guide."
Rose No letters?
Leslie (*reading another letter*) Just a bill I'm afraid.

Rose (*holding out the envelope she picked up earlier*) There's one here came the other day.

Leslie (*taking the envelope and opening it*) You don't mind me reading your mail?

Rose If it's a love letter give it back. I wouldn't ask if I could do it easily myself.

Leslie It's a card from — Vi. "Welcome home Rose, I'll be round when you've settled in. Love Vi."

Rose Oh dear.

Leslie She sounds a good friend.

Rose She means well. When I was in hospital she brought me this one-piece outfit, trousers and top together, a what-d'yer-call it — a ...

Leslie Jump suit?

Rose That's it, a lovely colour and very light. I was always complaining about the heat. Vi helped me into it and the nurses thought I looked a treat. I was happy as Larry, for a while.

Leslie Only a while?

Rose Until I needed the toilet. You ever been taken short in a jump suit?

Leslie Not lately.

Rose They got me down just in time. It made Elsie's day.

Leslie That's all your mail I'm afraid.

Rose You might as well go then.

Leslie There must be something else I can do.

Rose Like what?

Leslie Anything that might be useful, you tell me.

Rose I know, you can mow the lawn and do some weeding.

Leslie Gardening isn't in my brief Mrs Carlyle.

Rose So it's goodbye, because you're not going to vacuum, that's for sure.

Leslie Doesn't Danny want to see me? And I can see one thing that needs doing —your bed. (*He makes the bed during the following*)

Rose I suppose you wash and iron as well.

Leslie No, but I've done a few of these in my time.

Rose Do you cook?

Leslie You have to if you live alone.

Rose You're single then?
Leslie At the moment. How long were you married?
Rose Us? A lifetime.
Leslie I like the painting. Who did that?
Rose Mrs Picasso … It's what the boys called me, he was the only artist they knew.
Leslie You did this?
Rose We used to have holidays by the sea on a caravan site. I often got the paints out if I had while to myself.
Leslie You've got talent.
Rose Had maybe.

There is the sound of the front door closing

Danny (*off*) It's only me.
Rose That's Danny.

Danny enters. He is carrying a hand grip for Rose's toilet

(*Moving to Rose without seeing Leslie*) It's damp out there. (*He kisses Rose*) You all right?
Rose I'm OK. What's that you've got?
Danny The grip for your toilet.
Rose Good, I need that.
Danny I'll fix it while I'm here. I'll have a drink … (*He sees Leslie*) Oh, hallo, I didn't see you there.
Rose Danny meet the Home Help.
Danny What!
Leslie I'm Leslie Wilkinson, Mr Carlyle, pleased to meet you.
Danny (*to Rose*) You didn't tell me … (*To Leslie*) I'm sorry, I just assumed you were a woman.
Rose Isn't life full of surprises?
Danny And you're seeing to Mum over the weekend?
Leslie I should be, but …
Rose I've told him and I'm telling you Danny — no more visits.
Danny We'll talk about it later.
Rose Are you staying tonight?

Danny Sorry Mum, I ought to get back.
Leslie Shall I put the kettle on?
Rose No I'll do it.

Rose exits

Danny So, how do you find her?
Leslie She was all for throwing me out but I think I'm making headway.
Danny Stick with it, she'll come round. How long have you been doing this work?
Leslie About half an hour.
Danny Baptism of fire then. Your predecessor thought she was just a bloody nuisance.
Leslie I've dealt with some more problematic than your mother.
Danny Have you? Where?
Leslie I nursed in a hospital for a few years.
Danny You should know the score then. Mum can be a difficult customer. That's what they call then now don't they, in the market place. That's part of the new buzz language isn't it?
Leslie Not for those on the wards.
Danny Customers, clients, they'd like us all to be shopping around … You know, it would be more than useful if you could keep coming, for the next week anyway.
Leslie It's not really up to me, I go where I'm sent.
Danny She can't handle a succession of helpers, you're the third in two weeks.
Leslie The third!
Danny And last weekend — nobody. What do you think about her being here on her own?
Leslie I can't really say can I. She seems to be managing.
Danny Seems to be. The fact is she isn't. We can't have her and I can't keep driving down the motorway. I'm trying to manage a business.
Leslie Isn't here where she wants to be?
Danny Oh yes, except maybe back in her ward. She went in with a lung infection and they had to operate. Then they rang to say there'd been a set-back, she'd had a stroke in the theatre. Some setback!

Leslie How long was she in for?
Danny Six months. Long enough to like it.

There is the sound of breaking crockery from the kitchen

Rose (*off*) Bugger! Bloody thing!
Leslie I'll go.

Leslie exits to the kitchen

Danny looks at the made bed and takes off his jacket

Rose (*off*) Not you, I want Danny.
Leslie (*off*) Leave it, I'll clear this up.
Rose (*off*) Bring the coffee.

Rose enters with the trolley

Danny What happened?
Rose I dropped my mug. I was attached to that mug.
Danny Not attached enough Mum.
Rose (*sitting*) Smart arse.
Danny (*referring to the grip*) I'd better get on with this.
Rose Have your coffee first.
Danny Leslie seems capable enough.
Rose Give him a bucket of sand, he'll sing *The Desert Song*.
Danny He knows how to make a bed.
Rose I bet he can't sleep in it, I can't.
Danny It's the same bed you've had for years.
Rose But it wasn't down here was it.

The phone rings

Hallo … (*To Danny*) It's Daisy. (*Into the phone*) Hallo Daisy,
how are you love? … You what? … Had a fall. Oh dear, were you
hurt? … Were you hurt?

Leslie enters with a coffee jug and coffee cups etc. on a tray

But you're on the mend now. … Good. … Oh I'm all right. …
Leslie Shall I serve?

Danny nods

Rose (*into the phone*) Two weeks … Yes …
Danny They don't need a phone, Daisy only lives up the road.
Rose (*into the phone*) *Shut up, Danny!* … No love, I was talking to
Danny. … *Danny!* … I got your card Daisy, in hospital. … A long
time. No, no, *not two weeks, I've been home two weeks. You must
come down for a chat. … I'll say cheerio for now. Look after
yourself love.* … (*She hangs up*) Phew, she's hard work. Did you
hear her? She was under the doctor, broke her arm.
Danny There's life in the old girl yet then.
Leslie I've poured your coffee Mrs Carlyle.
Rose We've had some good times together.
Danny I'll fetch her down sometime Mum. Back in a minute.
Rose Drink your coffee.
Danny I need some things from the car.

Danny exits

Rose Always in a hurry, never sits or really talks, or listens. Not like
his brother Tom.
Leslie You have two sons?
Rose Did have. A soft fool his dad called him but he made me laugh.
If they operated on Danny tomorrow they wouldn't find his funny
bone. The other day I was telling him how I took a tumble in the
kitchen …
Leslie You fell over!
Rose No bones broken, I just lost my balance and found myself on
the floor. I wasn't hurt, but I couldn't get up. What I really needed
was a pair of strong arms. The young black nurse in the hospital,
she'd have done it, she lifted me a few times.
Leslie So what did you do?
Rose I crawled, as best I could, like a baby, giggling. I found the
broom, held it upright and hauled myself up. Tom would have

seen the funny side, all Danny said was "I'll get rid of that old lino." Not even a smile.

Leslie Perhaps you need a few more brooms around.

Rose He came back to live here after his marriage broke up. Then we had two burials in six months, old age and cancer. They're both together, in the same plot.

Leslie That must be a comfort.

Rose Makes no difference to them does it?

Leslie For you, I meant.

Rose It's in a lovely spot, top of a slope looking down. After we'd buried his dad Tom said, very seriously, "Mum, how many dead do you think are in here?" "I don't know," I said, "How many do you think?" And, smiling, he said ——

Leslie "I reckon they all are."

Rose How do you know that?

Leslie It's an old joke.

Rose Old or not, it was typical Tom. A few months later he was one of them.

Leslie I'll be going soon. I'll see you same time tomorrow.

Rose No you won't.

Leslie It's what I'm paid for.

Rose So take the money and run.

Leslie I can't do that.

Rose Oh suit yourself.

Leslie I was wondering — perhaps I ought to have a key.

Danny enters

Rose Key! I'm not giving you a key.

Leslie I'd save you a journey to the door, you might be having a sleep in your chair.

Rose Well don't come and I won't have to answer it.

Danny He should have a key Mum.

Rose No!

Danny There's a spare on the hook by the sink — take it.

Leslie exits

Rose *Danny!* You're in *my* house!
Danny I'm not worried about you dozing in the chair, it's you decomposing on the carpet. Somebody apart from me has got to have access.
Rose (*defeated*) What's the use. (*She stands*) Give me those cups.

Leslie returns

Danny I've done your toilet handle if you want to try it.
Rose I might need some water music.

Rose exits

Leslie I'm off now Mr Carlyle.
Danny You'll be in tomorrow?
Leslie I'll be here.
Danny You'd better have my phone numbers. (*He gives Leslie his card*)
Leslie (*reading the card*) You're in the car business?
Danny More out than in these days, too many cars and not enough business.
Leslie Isn't there still money in cars?
Danny Yes, so long as a new bypass doesn't put you into no-man's land... Are you a good nurse?
Leslie I used to think so.
Danny I used to think I was a good salesman.
Leslie Why not now?
Danny It just feels harder that's all. There's too many punters who feel they've been ripped off by dealers. The number's up for people like me anyway, soon people like you will be going to the Internet or the supermarket or direct to the factory. In a few years time I'll be another dinosaur, something you won't have to think about.
Leslie We're seeing changes too.
Danny Look, if you could do the next week ...
Leslie Like I said ...
Danny I'd make it worth your while, I don't mind paying for the extra hours.

Leslie I'll talk to them. One thing, your mother's medication …
Danny What about it?
Leslie I noticed she got three lots of pills.
Danny That's right.
Leslie Well, who sees that she takes them?
Danny I do and I remind her when I phone.
Leslie But when there's nobody here?
Danny Time will tell won't it? Anything else?
Leslie Just your signature to say I've been. (*He produces a form and hands it to Danny*)
Danny (*signing the form*) Keep up the good work.
Leslie We'll see.
Danny It really depends how you sell it to them, doesn't it?
Leslie (*taking the form*) Thank you.

Leslie exits

(*Off*) Bye, Mrs Carlyle.

The door slams, off

Danny picks up the phone and dials

Danny (*into the phone*) Hallo love it's me. … Much the same, she's got someone coming in but I'd better stay over anyway, perhaps have a few with the old crowd tonight. … Yes, I had a quick tour on the way down, I was impressed. … I know, I'll settle it before I leave. …
Rose (*off*) Danny.
Danny I've got to go, she's calling. I'll see you tomorrow. (*She puts the phone down*)
Rose (*off*) Danny.
Danny When they call the tune Mum, we all have to dance.
Rose (*off*) DANNY!
Danny All right! I'm coming …

The Lights slowly fade

SCENE 3

The same night

In the darkness, the flute melody plays slowly, becoming lost under the sound of a lapping tide, a sound which increases in intensity to be overtaken by a montage of discordant sounds and disembodied voices representing Rose's dream. We hear a child's cry; a thumping heart; strained breathing; then a cacophony of hospital noises rising to a climax. Then there is silence

Rose, who is sitting stationary on the edge of her bed, cries out, piercing the silence

Rose Nurse … nurse … nurse!

Danny enters and switches on the light

Danny It's all right, Mum, I'm here.
Rose (*bewildered*) Danny?
Danny I'm here. What is it?
Rose (*looking round at Danny*) Oh … Oh … I was dreaming … Then I woke — and …
Danny You're OK. I'm here.
Rose I didn't know where I was … I …
Danny There's a light, I showed you.
Rose I couldn't tell … I got out and I was frightened to move. I couldn't tell where the end of the bed was.
Danny Come on, let's get you back to bed.
Rose No, I'll sit for a while. I'm all right now. I didn't hear you come in.
Danny You were sound asleep. I sat and had a nightcap.
Rose What time is it now?
Danny Nearly four. You'd know if the old clock still chimed.
Rose That's been reprieved a few times. Tom was all for throwing it out but Dad wouldn't let him. He bought it off a stall in the fifties. I think it stopped when he did.

Danny Are you warm enough? Here, put your dressing gown round you.

Danny helps Rose into her dressing-gown

In the ward there was a lovely night nurse who brought me ice. I was always so hot in there. Ice and a kiss; I'd sleep after that ... Won't be long now.
Danny What?
Rose Dawn chorus. I used to listen to it upstairs, first one then the whole pack of them singing away. I'd draw back the curtains and look out into the garden and the trees and the early sun. Sometimes I had another doze or else I'd just rest, waiting for the milk float or the clatter of the paper in the door. For weeks after Tom died I looked in his room to see if he was there. Even when I saw the empty bed I told myself he'd be in.
Danny I can remember both of us giggling our way up the stairs early in the morning after some party or other, scared to wake you and Dad. We'd discovered it was easier to come in at dawn than after midnight.
Rose Do you think I didn't know, of course I did. When are you off?
Danny Early.
Rose You'll be down again soon?
Danny When I can. I need to tell you something Mum ...

Rose fumbles in the pocket of her dressing-gown

Are you listening?
Rose I thought I had a tissue.
Danny (*taking a tissue from the trolley*) Here.

Danny gives Rose the tissue

(*Studying Rose*) I'm worried about you, you're not looking after yourself, I can tell.
Rose Nonsense.
Danny You're not eating or sleeping well, you're falling over ...

Rose I wasn't hurt.

Danny What would you have done tonight if I wasn't here? What happens tomorrow night?

Rose I shouldn't have told you.

Danny I can't keep coming down any more.

Rose You don't have to during the week, just phone.

Danny No you don't understand. We're moving. The company's moving and I'm going with it.

Rose Where?

Danny They're closing the showroom, the site's no longer viable. They've asked me to go up to Glasgow as Sales Manager for a new one opening up. I can't turn it down.

Rose Glasgow.

Danny I'm lucky they asked me, they could have recruited locally.

Rose All of you? The girls as well?

Danny When their courses have finished they'll be flying the nest anyway. I'm starting in a couple of weeks. We think we've got a buyer for our house and when it's sorted Linda will join me and we'll start looking for another property.

Rose It's all fixed then.

Danny I couldn't tell you until I knew it was happening. The point is you can't live alone in this house any more.

Rose This house! My home you mean!

Danny I shouldn't have to spell it out.

Rose I'm managing Danny. Give me time, it'll get easier.

Danny I think you don't really believe that … There's a residential home overlooking a lovely part of the river, with trees and a flower garden …

Rose You've been there have you?

Danny Only for a quick visit. The rooms are really nice, so are the staff …

Rose You'd better get your name on the waiting list now then.

Danny They're having an open day next week. I thought we could have a trip out so you could see what it's like.

Rose I don't need to.

Danny It wouldn't do you any harm to have a look.

Rose You're flogging a dead horse! (*She smiles*)

Danny What's amusing?

Rose I seem to remember somebody else saying that … This is the only home I'm going to reside in and when I leave here all the care you'll need to think about are a few flowers by our headstone.

Danny That's it then is it?

Rose That's it.

Danny Perhaps Leslie will turn up trumps.

Rose I wouldn't put your eggs in his basket.

Danny But you quite like him don't you?

Rose At least he lets me talk. With Brenda I had to listen.

Danny I'm back to bed; so should you be.

Rose I won't be long.

Danny (*taking Rose's hand*) You OK?

Rose I'm O.K.

A single bird sings throughout the following

Do you hear that? It's Saturday isn't it?

Danny It was.

Rose You know what happens now … Listen, do you hear?

Danny What?

Rose Noisy key in the lock … Door opening, easing shut … Jackets on stand …

Danny Shoes off …

Rose Whispers on the stairs, giggles on the landing … Into bedroom …

Danny Ties off, shirts off, empty pockets, trousers over chair …

Rose Socks on floor …

Danny Stumble into bed …

Rose Fresh sheets, friendly pillows …

Danny "Goodnight Tom." "Night Danny." Heads down …

Rose Rest easy now …

Danny kisses Rose and leaves

…the boys are in.

The single birdsong swells into a chorus

Rose sits listening

The birdsong and the Lights slowly fade

Scene 4

The same. Sunday morning

There are a brandy glass and a half-full bottle of brandy by the telephone. There are a skirt and blouse on the rail and a pair of Rose's shoes on the floor nearby

The Lights come up. Rose is asleep in her chair wearing her dressing-gown

The doorbell rings. Rose doesn't wake up. The front door shuts

Leslie (*off*) Good morning Mrs Carlyle, it's me, Leslie.

> *Leslie enters, limping slightly and holding a bloodied handkerchief to a damaged hand*

Leslie sees Rose and for a moment suspects the worst. He bends towards her. She shifts a little. Leslie turns away, relieved, and rubs his damaged leg. Rose's eyes open with Leslie's bloodied hand in her full view. She jolts in the chair, looks closer at his hand and then up to his face

Rose I hope you're not staining my carpet!
Leslie No, I don't think so.
Rose How did you get in?
Leslie I had a key, remember. I'm sorry about this, I've had an accident.
Rose What kind of accident?
Leslie On the way here … I'm all right, just a bit shaken up.
Rose Were you mugged?
Leslie In a manner of speaking.

Rose Ring the local paper, they love muggings. Where was it?
Leslie Over by the Parade, coming round the circle.
Rose That's a relief.
Leslie What!
Rose At least it wasn't in my street.
Leslie It was a lorry with a trailer. Just ignored me and smashed the bike up. It's out there with a twisted fork and caved-in wheel and gear … Shit!
Rose Pardon!
Leslie I just feel so bloody angry.
Rose Call that angry! Go on lad, better out than in, let's hear it, more.
Leslie Fuck it then!
Rose Pathetic. Shout it out, get rid of it.
Leslie BASTARD! FUCK YOU, YOU FUCKING, FUCKING BASTARD!

There is silence. Leslie looks embarrassed. Rose smiles at him

That wasn't very professional was it?
Rose I've done much the same more than once lately.
Leslie You didn't have an audience.
Rose (*pointing to the wall*) You can bet your life I did.
Leslie (*more embarrassed*) Christ! I could do with a plaster.
Rose You're sure that's all?
Leslie It's just a cut and a few grazes.
Rose You should know. Now then plasters, plasters. There used to be some in the kitchen drawer.
Leslie I ought to wash myself down a bit.
Rose There's soap and towel in my toilet. And make some tea while you're at it, it's good for shock is tea. That's what I gave the poor old thing when he came back after being hit by a car.
Leslie Your husband was run over?
Rose No, he was drunk, the dog was run over.

Leslie exits

I think it was only the dog.

The phone rings. Rose answers it

(*Into the phone*) Hallo ... Hallo Daisy, how are you today? ... Yes I know you told me yesterday ... I'm all right ... No I was in hospital, I've been home a couple of weeks ... Can you come down? We'll have a good talk ... When I what? ... No I told you, I've already been ...(*To herself*) Oh Daisy. (*Into the phone*) I'll speak to you soon love. (*She replaces the receiver and sees the remains of Danny's nightcap — the brandy. She holds the bottle up and notes that it is not empty. To Leslie, loudly*) You all right in there? Shout if you want help. (*She pours herself a brandy, one-handed, and puts the drink to one side*)

Leslie enters with two mugs of tea. He has a plaster on his hand

Rose All done?
Leslie I shall be sore for a while.
Rose You'll mend.
Leslie I shouldn't really be doing this.
Rose What should you be doing?
Leslie Looking after you I suppose. I see you're not dressed yet.
Rose I had a restless night. Now then, I've got a little something for you.
Leslie For me?
Rose For a special occasion. It's not every day you're run over.
Leslie Wait. I've got something for you. It's in the kitchen.

Leslie exits

Rose moves the brandy glass closer

Leslie enters with a compartmentalized tablet dispenser

Leslie I want your attention for a few minutes.
Rose (*holding the brandy out to Leslie*) Get this down you first.
Leslie What is it?
Rose Brandy.

Leslie It's a bit early for brandy.
Rose Not in your condition.

Leslie takes the glass and puts it aside

Leslie This is a pill dispenser.
Rose Pill dispenser! That's what you've got for me.
Leslie Look, it has days of the week and each day has compartments.
Rose I always gave Stan his pills, he didn't know which ones to take.
Leslie This'll help you to know yours.
Rose I could have given him anything, he wouldn't have been any the wiser.
Leslie I think the doctors would have. I'll load it up for you, a week's supply. I've already done today's and tomorrow's. The bedtime ones are bigger than the others, can you see?

Rose peers at the dispenser

You need to take them in the right order. So if it's morning, you just push it open a little like this (*he demonstrates*), shake them on to your hand, pop them in and wash them down.
Rose I did some "popping" in hospital — into bed, out of bed, on to a trolley, into a chair. As for pills, I daren't tell you where they popped some of those.
Leslie They all count, even the small ones. You can forget about the bottles, just tell Danny to refill it. Have you got all that?
Rose And in the morning I start on the next day's.
Leslie Exactly. So have you had your morning pills yet?
Rose I'll take them now with my tea. (*She takes the dispenser, opens it and raises it to her eye. She turns it over, releasing a show of pills on to the trolley*)
Leslie No! You ——
Rose What happened there?
Leslie You can't turn it upside down, you've got to put them on to your hand. Here, swallow these. (*He gathers the pills up*) Not to worry, I'll load it again.

Rose (*taking the pills*) I'd better stick to the bottles. Go on have your drink.

Leslie I think I'll leave it.

Rose Go on, you need it.

Leslie No, thanks, anyway.

Rose It'll do you more good than harm.

Leslie I'd rather not.

Rose Nobody's looking, it's only a small drop.

Leslie (*vehemently*) *I said no for Christ's sake!*

Pause

Rose My word … What's rattled your cage?

Leslie I don't drink Mrs Carlyle.

Rose Don't or can't?

Leslie For me there's no such thing as a small drop.

Rose Well, aren't you a dark horse? I can't blame you for that. God knows I've tried hard enough to hang on to some small scrap of privacy.

Leslie It's something I'd rather not advertise.

Rose How long have you been … ?

Leslie Dry? A couple of months.

Rose Early days then. Were you really a nurse?

Leslie And married to one. Still am on paper.

Rose Is this why you left?

Leslie I'd become — dangerous.

Rose They said that?

Leslie More or less. I couldn't be trusted with patient care.

Rose You needn't tell me any more.

Leslie If anything it helps … We'd been drifting apart for months. It didn't make things easier being on different shifts, constantly going in opposite directions. I began drinking more in company and taking an extra supply home; I didn't notice or care how much it was taking hold. She did, but I wouldn't listen so she gave up — then there was nothing to listen to. The crunch came when I lost my licence and she said she was leaving. That night I had a skinful, but next morning I managed to drag myself into work on the bus.

The ward seemed busier than usual. My first job was to set up a syringe-driver for a cancer patient. It's a fairly simple apparatus that feeds a flow of diamorphine into the body; I'd done it a hundred times. I noted the prescribed dosage, estimated the correct amount of flow, adjusted the millilitres-per-hour setting and got the student nurse who was with me to check my calculations and the setting. She must've thought it was an unnecessary formality; I'd made it obvious it was a procedure I was familiar with. Anyway she okayed it and we went off to do other things. Not long after, all hell broke loose. The patient was unconscious; I'd miss-set the flow and given him an overdose. They got to him just in time. I was hauled in front of my Manager who gave me a severe reprimand and, before sending me home, some friendly advice and a telephone number. When I got back she'd moved out. I had a last stiff drink reading her note, and then I made a phone call.

Rose So now?

Leslie Now? I'm working at it, with help.

Rose My Tom could have taken a leaf out of your book. I'm sorry for your trouble. People have said that to me enough times. What's your wife's name?

Leslie Her parents had been dancers. They named her after a film star.

Rose Ginger?

Leslie Cyd, after Cyd Charisse.

Rose I remember her, she had lovely legs. That must have confused your wedding, the bride called Cyd and the groom Leslie.

Leslie Not just the wedding.

Rose We used to cut a dash on the dance floor; none of your shaking about, the real McCoy. Do you think you'll ever get back together?

Leslie I've had a letter from a solicitor, she's not interested in a reconciliation.

Rose She couldn't tell you herself?

Leslie She wants to keep her distance.

Rose Why? Did you threaten her?

Leslie No — but just once … I can't even remember what it was about except that something snapped. We were never the same afterwards. I tried to talk us through it, promised I'd quit. I couldn't have sounded very convincing. All she got was the drunk's dream, regrets for yesterday and resolutions for tomorrow but never for today.

Rose You've got to talk to her again.

Leslie It's too late.

Rose Only if you want it to be.

Leslie She's probably met someone by now.

Rose You youngsters! Why don't you write "maybe" or "probably" into the marriage service? For better or for worse doesn't seem to mean anything these days. If you know marriage is so easy to get out of how can you think seriously about getting into it?

Leslie How many of your years were better or worse?

Rose All couples have their bad times. And Stan never raised his hand to me. Mind you, he was only five foot four so if he had I'd have flattened him … Where are you living?

Leslie In a bedsit, not far.

Rose Bedsit. That must be lonely.

Leslie It'll do for a while.

Rose I've got rooms I haven't been into for months. Enough of this. Are you in a hurry?

Leslie No.

Rose What's the day like?

Leslie It's fine.

Rose Good. Let's go out.

Leslie Out! How?

Rose You'll see. I'd better have a quick wash and get dressed.

Leslie Do you need help?

Rose Just for the zip and buttons. Upstairs there's something Danny brought in. I told Brenda to take it out of my sight; you can fetch it down.

Leslie You want me to go upstairs.

Rose You can't miss it, she's put it on the landing. And while you're there, look in my bedroom in the back. I had a box with all sorts of bits and pieces; I can't believe Danny's thrown it away.

Leslie exits

Rose stands, selects a skirt and blouse from the clothes rail and puts them on the trolley. She studies Leslie's brandy glass

(*Scolding herself quietly*) Oh you silly woman!

Rose exits, pushing the trolley

Leslie returns with a cardboard box file and a wheelchair

Leslie places the box on the bed and unfolds the wheelchair. He checks the tyres, sits in the chair and wheels himself around the room, taking in the mantelpiece. He sits still, thinking

Rose enters wearing the blouse and skirt

Rose Action stations. I hope you know how to push that.
Leslie I ought to.
Rose Some of them thought I was a sack of King Edward's. Do me up please.
Leslie (*buttoning Rose's blouse*) Where are we going?
Rose Not far. Thank you. Shoes please. Over there somewhere. (*She gestures*)
Leslie (*finding Rose's shoes*) Shall I?
Rose Please.

Leslie fits Rose's shoes during the following

This was my coming-home outfit. It felt strange having these on. Now what else?
Leslie Your hair could do with a comb.
Rose Good for you. Fetch my coat and I'll find the brush.

Leslie exits

Rose finds the brush on the lower shelf of the trolley

Leslie enters with Rose's coat

Rose holds the brush out to Leslie; he takes it, and brushes Rose's hair during the following

Leslie (*as he brushes*) Who played the flute?
Rose That was Stan's. He was a good musician in his day. And at bedtime magic with the boys, the Pied Piper with two imps dancing up the stairs behind him. (*She stands*)

Leslie helps Rose into her coat

Thank you. How do I look?
Leslie I think you'll turn a head or two.
Rose I will when you push me out in this. (*She settles into the wheelchair*) I hope next door's watching. I've just had a thought. Are you on this Community Service?
Leslie No Mrs Carlyle.
Rose Well you are now, a double dose. I warn you, you're in for a punishing hour.
Leslie Where are we off to?
Rose Up the road, to see Daisy. And if you're going to be my toy-boy stop calling me Mrs Carlyle. Do you hear me?
Leslie I hear you Rose. You're the boss.
Rose Am I? That makes a change.
Leslie All set then?
Rose All set.

They exit

The front door slams

The Lights fade

SCENE 5

A week later. Early evening

The Lights come up

Leslie (*off*) Rose.

  Leslie enters, wearing overalls

  Rose.
Rose (*off*) Wait!

Leslie paces the floor, smiling

There is the sound of the toilet flushing

Leslie (*calling to Rose*) Everything all right?
Rose (*making her way to chair*) It's no good you calling me when
  I'm in there, nothing happens any faster.
Leslie How are you feeling now?
Rose I'll live.
Leslie (*feeling her forehead*) You're a bit hot.
Rose I'm all right, don't fuss.
Leslie I think in the morning I'll ring the doctor.
Rose It'll pass, now what do you want?
Leslie I've got something to give you. Close your eyes and open
  your hand.
Rose Have you been to the chemist again?
Leslie Do as you're told.
Rose Typical nurse. (*She closes her eyes*)

Leslie produces an old wallet and puts it in Rose's hand

  What's this?
Leslie Open it.
Rose I recognise this. It's one of Stan's wallets; I gave him this.

Leslie Look what's inside.

Rose (*opening the wallet*) I knew it!

Leslie Here, let me. (*He takes out dozens of notes*)

Rose How much is there?

Leslie Must be hundreds. I was looking for sandpaper in the garage. It was in the back of a drawer in his workbench.

Rose I guessed he was hoarding money, we weren't spending it. I bet there's more somewhere.

Leslie You're not hoarding money are you Rose?

Rose Only in the bank. Danny's opened an account for me. Tom often puzzled over what his dad was trying to tell him on the last visit. He thought he heard him say something about a "funny marriage". My eye, it was money in the garage he was on about.

Leslie Shall we count it?

Rose It's not going to change my life now is it?

Leslie The sooner it's in your account the better.

Rose We'll drop it in tomorrow. How are you getting on up there?

Leslie I'm ready to paint; all the hard work's done.

Rose You're sure you want to do it?

Leslie I like to keep busy.

Rose I bet it was hard work. Tom used to spend hours in there smoking himself to … . Anyway I don't think it was Weights or Woodbines.

Leslie And you're happy with the colour scheme?

Rose It's your room now Leslie, you can do as you like.

Leslie Rose it's a room in your house; sooner or later I'll be moving on.

Rose I know.

Leslie And about my rent …

Rose Your what?

Leslie I ought to give you something.

Rose You do, and I'm not exactly short of a penny am I?

Leslie I'm sure Danny would expect me to.

Rose No he wouldn't.

Leslie I ought to get changed.

Rose What do you talk about at your meetings?

Leslie (*sitting and removing his shoes*) The past, the present, anything worth sharing.

Rose Your women?
Leslie Sometimes. There's women members.
Rose The patient you had a problem with: how old was he?
Leslie Somewhere in his sixties.
Rose Did you know much about him?
Leslie He hadn't been on the ward long.
Rose You could have been doing him a favour.
Leslie I wasn't in nursing to do happy accidents.

Leslie exits

Rose looks at the notes and wallet

Rose Oh Stanley, you silly, silly bugger!

Rose goes through the contents of the box file, using her reading glass. The box contains old photos, letters, cards, policies and other items; most are given a cursory look. She finds a box of watercolour paints and pays it close attention

Leslie enters

Rose Look at this, my old paint box. I haven't seen it for years.
Leslie It's been well used. A bit of history there Rose.
Rose Needs a few refills now. Such lovely names the colours; cadmium yellow — burnt sienna — hooker's green. Why hooker's I don't know.
Leslie You still remember them.
Rose This was a good friend to me. Do you know what this one is? When Tom was little he stood at my elbow once watching me paint and mixing the colours — a bit of this, a touch of that. "What are you doing now?" he said. "Making rose madder," I said. I can still hear him laughing himself silly. It became a family joke.
Leslie Did you ever sell any?
Rose I wouldn't have known what to ask. It was just something I did for pleasure. A lot was done here in this room. I used to paint myself into a scene, imagine I was on a cliff or hill looking out to sea, or in a wood surrounded by flowers. "Who's the small girl?"

they'd say. I never told them it was me ... Go on, you'll be late.
Leslie I think I'll give it a miss, I don't have to go.
Rose Yes you do. Don't worry about me, I'll not be long out of bed.
   You've got your key?
Leslie I shouldn't be late. I enjoyed today Rose.
Rose Did you Leslie? Me too.
Leslie It's going to be fine tomorrow. I thought we could take a trip
   out, maybe have some lunch and visit the grave if you're up to it.
Rose I'd like that. (*She regards the* wallet) We'll have it on Stan.
   He can pay for a cab too.
Leslie Sleep well.
Rose I'm tired; I think I will tonight.

We hear the front door closing

*Rose waits for the door to close, makes her way to the bedside and
stands looking towards the painting, which she cannot now see in
detail. She sits on the bed, remembering ...*

Rose Chinese white ... vermilion ... burnt umber ... scarlet lake ...
   rose madder ...

The Lights fade slowly

SCENE 6

Two months later

*The room is bare apart from the objects on the mantelpiece, the
watercolour and the bed*

*The Lights come up. Danny is stripping the bed, stowing the bedding
into a large hold-all*

The doorbell rings

Danny exits to answer the door

Danny (*off*) Leslie!
Leslie (*off*) Hallo Danny.
Danny (*off*) Come in.

Leslie enters

Leslie I saw the car, thought I'd stop by.
Danny How are you?
Leslie Still above ground. You're busy I see.
Danny I'm almost through. The new people are in this afternoon. The bed's staying, but they won't want this lot.
Leslie How's things in the north?
Danny We like it, it's got a lot to offer, not to mention the price of property. Thank God there were no hiccups with this one.
Leslie Who's coming in?
Danny A young family. Mum would have been pleased about that.
Leslie It's a good garden for kids.
Danny What are you doing with yourself?
Leslie Getting back to nursing full time.
Danny Good, I'm glad to hear it. I don't think I ever really thanked you for all you did for Mum, and for me.
Leslie It wasn't all one way, I was happy living here.
Danny I can't help feeling I should have done more. Perhaps moved down here or even in with her.
Leslie Could you see Rose sharing her house with another woman?
Danny Maybe not, but that doesn't stop me feeling guilty. When Dad went I blessed him for making it so easy and when Tom died I was walking a tightrope trying to balance my needs against Mum's. I'm just grateful she had your care. (*He takes the painting down*)
Leslie (*moving to the mantelpiece*) We shared a lot Danny. I'll miss her.
Danny If you'd looked in earlier there may have been something you could have had.
Leslie (*examining clock*) I can't think of anything.
Danny You're welcome to that, I was going to leave it. Not much was any use to me. There was one thing I would have liked. In the

kitchen there used to be a long cupboard with a single door. We grew up with it. On the inside of the door, running from the top in small, neat writing, were entries in pencil dating back to when Tom was born. There must have been hundreds of them — outings we'd had, when we started school, passed the eleven-plus, Tom's first suit, my first car, weddings, births, all with dates, all happy times. We never saw Mum writing them but whenever we came over we'd take a peek at the new entries. There were always some. Then one time after we'd been on holiday we all came over for Sunday dinner and the kitchen had been redeco-rated. It was just a paint job but it looked very smart. I saw the cupboard shining with a gloss yellow and went over to it, just to see … It had all gone. He'd painted it all out, wiped it. She never started it again, kept it all inside, I suppose. Well, that's it then. I can't offer you a drink, I'm afraid.

Leslie I have to go, anyway.

Danny Are you still in the saddle?

Leslie And making sure I stay there.

They shake hands

Goodbye Danny.

Danny So long old son. Good luck, and if you ever find yourself stuck in Glasgow and ——

Leslie Want a good deal on a car ——

Danny Dan's your man.

Leslie I'll remember that. You know, that old clock might be worth more than you think.

Leslie exits

Danny reflects on Leslie's last comment for a second then exits to the kitchen. He returns with a large spray of flowers and a card

Danny places the flowers and card below the mantelpiece. He rises, tucks the flute under his arm, then studies the clock's face. He turns the clock round and opens its back to find — a wad of notes

Danny You cunning old bugger! (*He pockets the money and gathers his luggage, retaining the clock*)

The flute melody begins softly

Danny takes a last look around the room and leaves

The Lights and music fade out

FURNITURE AND PROPERTY LIST

SCENE 1

On stage: *On mantelpiece*: Old carriage clock with wad of banknotes inside, flute, family photos

Single made-up bed
Clothes rail
Bedside cabinet. *On it*: light
TV
Chair
Table. *On it*: telephone
Framed watercolour beach scene for Danny

SCENE 2

Set: Dressing-gown on end of bed
Un-make bed
Scatter pills on floor

Off stage: Trolley. *On it*: slice of buttered toast, mug of tea, long arm gripper rod, reading glass, box of tissues, pills, envelope, jumble of objects (**Rose**)
Bottle of milk, loaf of bread (**Leslie**)
Mail, newspaper (**Leslie**)
Tray of tea items and biscuits (**Leslie**)
Hand grip for the toilet (**Danny**)
Tray of coffee jug and cups etc. (**Leslie**)

Personal: **Leslie**: bag containing cycle clips, cap and form

SCENE 3

Strike: All additional props from SCENE 2 except trolley, tissues, long arm gripper rod, and reading glass

No additional props

SCENE 4

Set: Brandy glass, half-full bottle of brandy
Skirt and blouse for **Rose** on rail
Pair of shoes for **Rose**
Hairbrush for **Rose**

Off stage: Two mugs of tea (**Leslie**)
Compartmentalized tablet dispenser containing pills (**Leslie**)
Cardboard box file containing old photos, letters, cards, policies, watercolour paints etc.; wheelchair (**Leslie**)

Personal: **Leslie**: blooded handkerchief; then plaster

SCENE 5

Strike: All additional props from Scene 4 except cardboard box file

Off stage: Old wallet containing banknotes (**Leslie**)

SCENE 6

Strike: All props except mantelpiece objects, watercolour and paint

On stage: Large holdall for **Danny**

Off stage: Large spray of flowers, card (**Danny**)

LIGHTING PLOT

Practical fittings required: bedside light
Interior. The same throughout

Scene 1

Cue 1   Music   (Page 1)
Bring up general interior lighting

Cue 2   **Danny** exits   (Page 1)
Fade lights

Scene 2

Cue 3   When ready   (Page 2)
Bring up general interior lighting

Cue 4   **Danny**: "All right, I'm coming.."   (Page 19)
Slowly fade lights

Scene 3

Cue 5   **Danny** switches on the light   (Page 20)
Bring up general interior lighting

Cue 6   **Rose** sits listening   (Page 24)
Fade lights

Scene 4

Cue 7   When ready   (Page 24)
Bring up general interior lighting

Cue 8   Front door slams   (Page 32)
Fade lights

SCENE 5

Cue 9   When ready   (Page 33)
            Bring up general interior lighting

Cue 10   **Rose**: " ... rose madder ..."   (Page 36)
            Slowly fade lights

SCENE 6

Cue 11   When ready   (Page 36)
            Bring up general interior lighting

Cue 12   **Danny** exits   (Page 39)
            Fade lights

EFFECTS PLOT

Cue 12	**Leslie**: "Bye, Mrs Carlyle." *Door slams, off*	(Page 19)
Cue 13	When ready *Flute melody / lapping tide, increasing in intensity / discordant sounds and disembodied voices / child's cry / thumping heart / strained breathing / cacophony of hospital noises rising to climax (See p. 20)*	(Page 20)
Cue 14	**Rose**: "I'm OK." *Single bird sings; continuous*	(Page 23)
Cue 15	**Rose**: " … the boys are in." *Birdsong swells into a chorus*	(Page 23)
Cue 16	**Rose** sits listening; pause *Fade birdsong slowly*	(Page 24)
Cue 17	Scene 3 is established *Doorbell rings; pause; front door closes*	(Page 24)
Cue 18	**Rose**: "I think it was only the dog." *Phone rings*	(Page 25)
Cue 19	**Leslie** and **Rose** exit *Front door slams*	(Page 32)
Cue 20	**Leslie** paces the floor, smiling *Toilet flushes*	(Page 33)
Cue 21	Scene 6 is established *Doorbell rings*	(Page 36)
Cue 22	**Danny** gathers his luggage *Flute melody, softly*	(Page 39)
Cue 23	**Danny** exits *Music fades*	(Page 39)